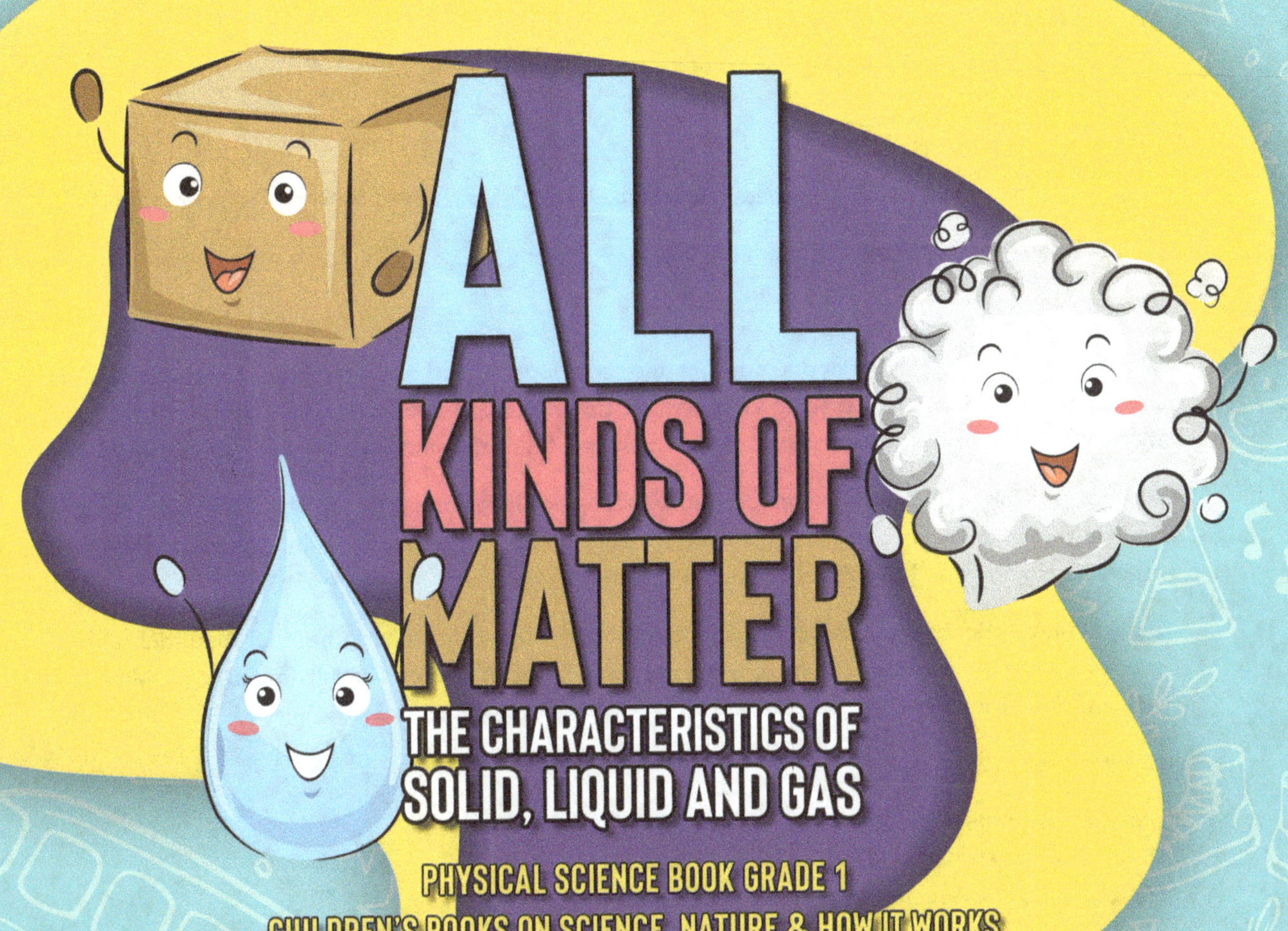

ALL
KINDS OF
MATTER
THE CHARACTERISTICS OF
SOLID, LIQUID AND GAS
PHYSICAL SCIENCE BOOK GRADE 1
CHILDREN'S BOOKS ON SCIENCE, NATURE & HOW IT WORKS

BABY PROFESSOR
EDUCATION KIDS

See the world in pictures. Build your knowledge in style.
www.speedypublishing.com

TABLE OF CONTENTS

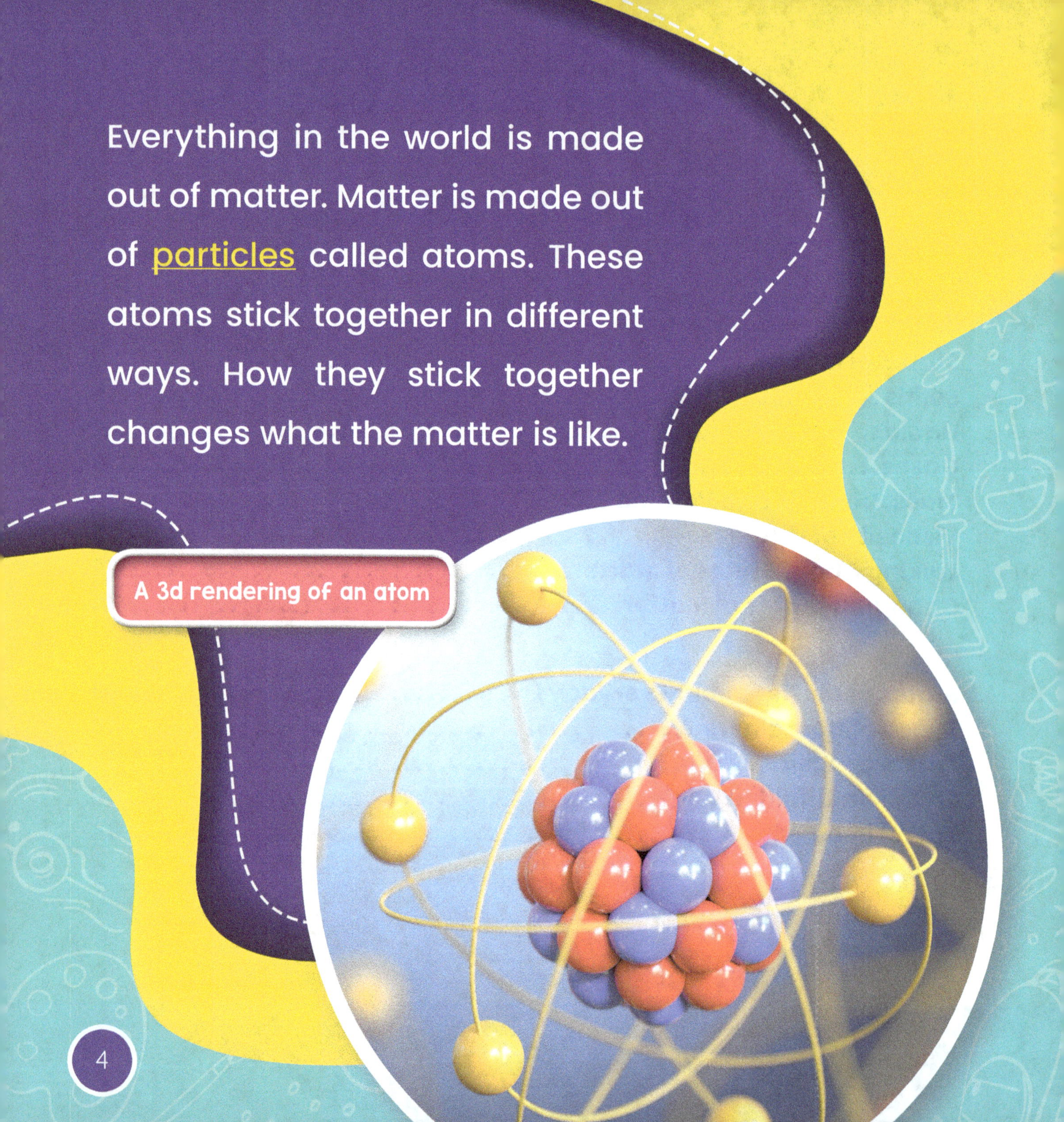

Everything in the world is made out of matter. Matter is made out of _particles_ called atoms. These atoms stick together in different ways. How they stick together changes what the matter is like.

Matter can come in three well-known, <u>unique</u> states: Solid, liquid, and gas. These states also affect what we do in our everyday lives.

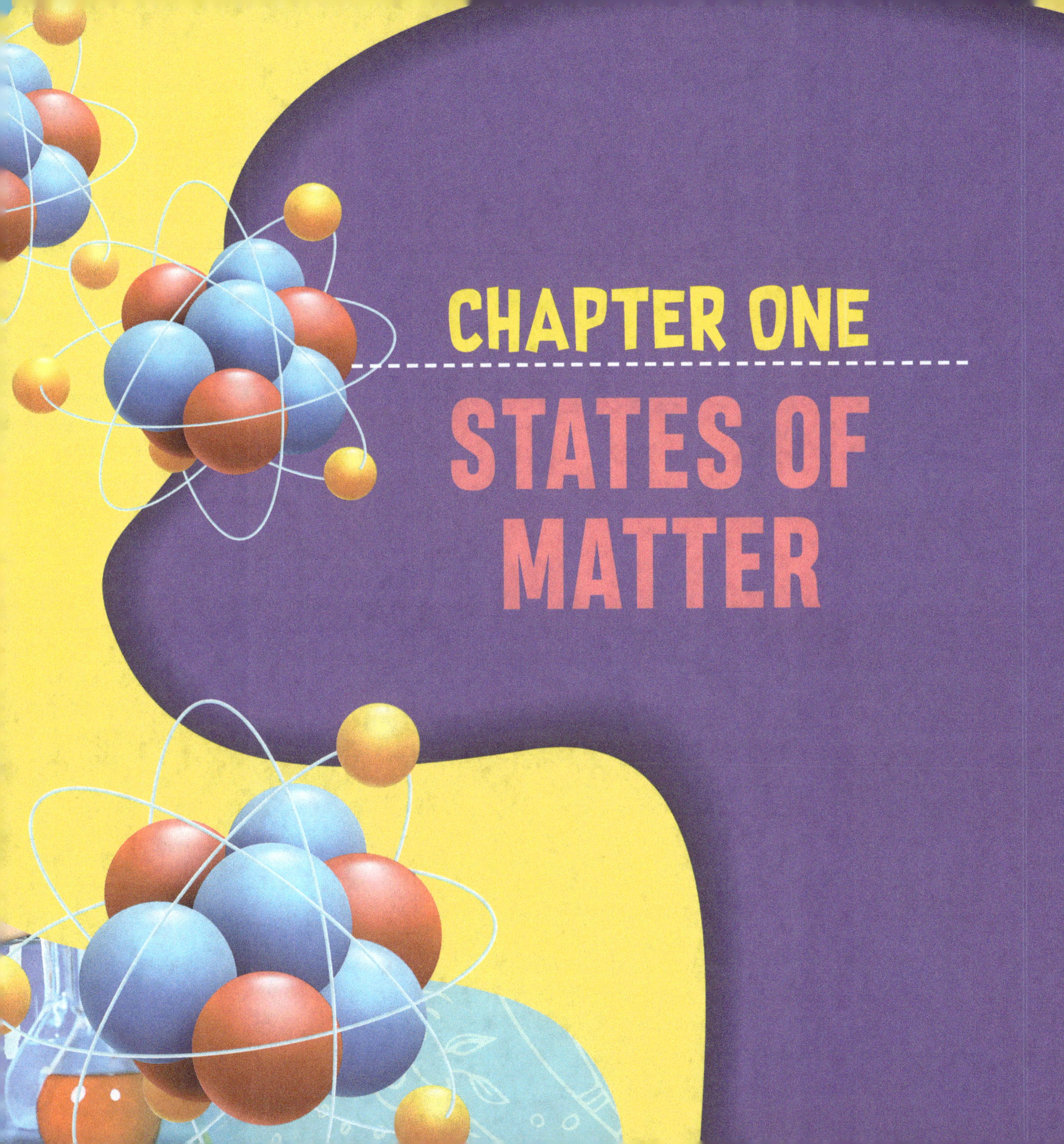

CHAPTER ONE
STATES OF MATTER

A comparison of the atoms in solid, liquid and gas.

Atoms are the smallest whole particle that everything is made from. Atoms stick together with special bonds. Solids, liquids, and gases change their states because of these bonds.

SOLIDS

In solids, atoms are packed together really close. They cannot move very much. That is why solids have a fixed shape and volume. Volume is how much space matter takes up.

It does not matter what kind of container solids are put in. It will keep the same shape. You also cannot force a bigger solid into a smaller <u>container</u>.

Solids are also usually hard or firm. Wood, metal, and cardboard are solids you can find in everyday life.

LIQUIDS

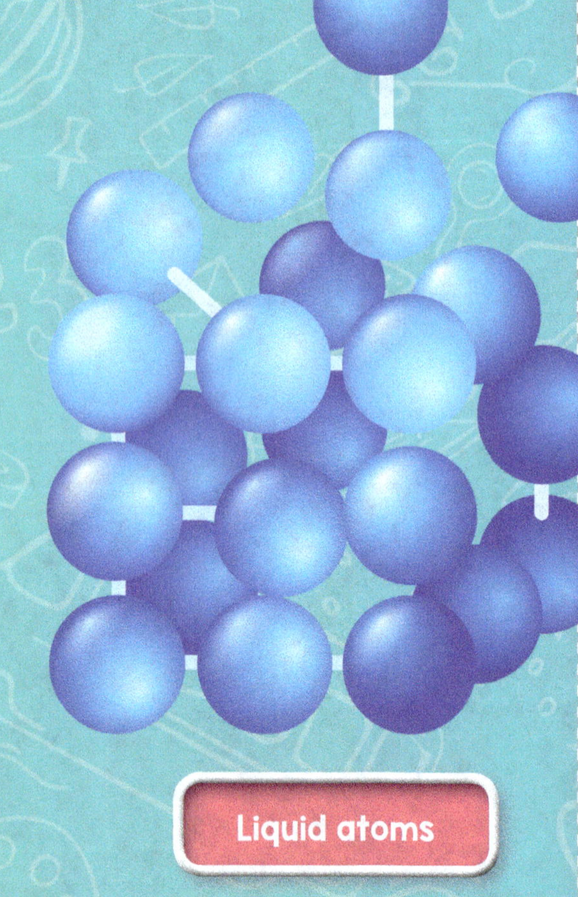

The atoms in liquids are not quite as close or as tight as in solids. The atoms can slip and slide over each other. This means liquids can change their shape easily.

If you put liquid in a container, it will change shape to fit the container. If you spill a liquid, it will spread into a puddle.

Liquids will keep the same volume though. Water, milk, ketchup, and juice are all liquids.

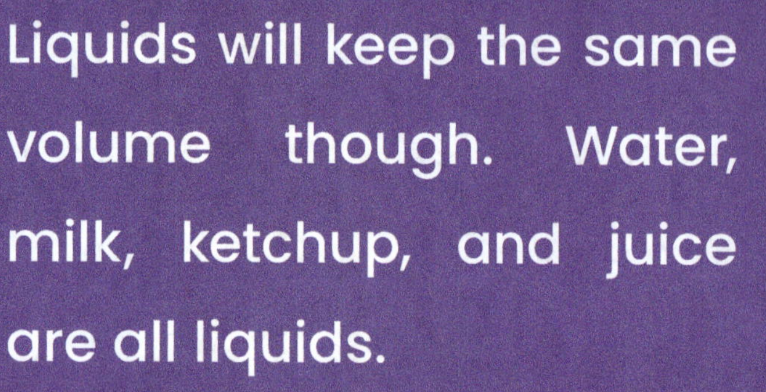

GASES

Atoms are quite far apart with gases. They are so far apart that they can move around a lot.

Gases change shape easily. In a container, gases spread out to match the volume inside. This means the volume of gas can change. You can see this happen when you blow up a balloon or pump air into a tire.

You can change the shape and
volume of gases easily.

When you smell things, it is because gas has spread around the room and into your nose!

Many gases are invisible. The oxygen you breathe in is a gas. The air around you is made up of various gases.

The air you breathe is made up of different gases.

MASS, DENSITY, AND VOLUME

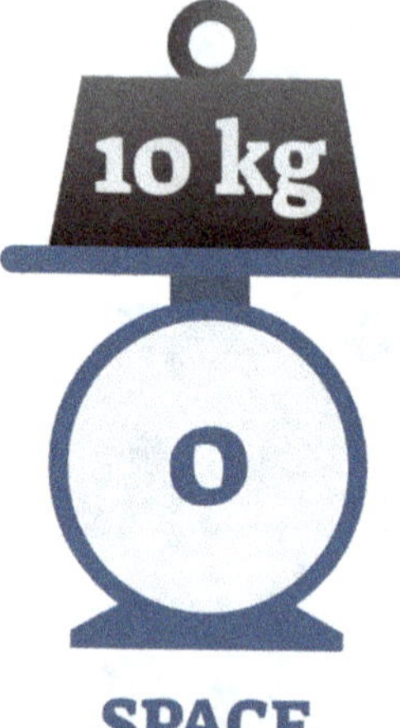

MASS is constant

WEIGHT is variable

Mass is how much matter something has. Mass is often confused with weight. Weight is how much gravity pulls on an object. Objects with more mass are heavier. This is because gravity pulls more on them.

To test mass, you can use balancing scales. These are a bit like a see-saw. Put a weight with a mass you know on one side. Put the objects with mass you do not know on the other side. When the balancing scales are equal, the mass is the same on both sides. If it is not, the heavier side will sink down. Since gravity pulls the same on both sides, it does not matter where in Space you use the scales. You could use them on the Moon. It would still work even though there is less gravity there.

A balancing scale is not dependent on gravity that's why it works even on the moon.

Mass can be measured in grams, kilograms or pounds.

Mass is typically weighed in grams or kilograms in Science. People might also use pounds in everyday life to measure mass.

Mass is not the same as volume. Something can take up a lot of space, but not have much matter. Volumes are typically measured in liters or milliliters, or squared meters and centimeters in Science. In everyday life, they can also be measured in units like ounces, gallons, or square inches.

Density is related to both volume and mass. Density is how much mass is in a certain space. The more tightly packed together matter is into a space, the denser it is.

Imagine pulling several tissues out of a tissue box. There is now less mass in the space inside the tissue box. This means that the box is not as dense. If you put in more tissues, there would be more mass in that same space. This means the box becomes denser.

VISCOSITY OF LIQUIDS

Some liquids spread out more easily than others when they spill or are poured. These liquids can seem more solid than others. They do not change shape as easily or quickly. The more viscous something is, the less it flows. Honey, for instance, is more viscous than water.

Honey is viscous, which means it does not spread quickly.

Spilled oil and coffee

You can test viscosity yourself. Once a liquid is spilled, watch how far it moves. When it stops, measure the distance it moved with a ruler. The liquid that moves the least is the most viscous. The opposite of viscous is fluid.

You can also record the distances in a tally chart. Later you can put the information into a bar graph. Graphs and charts allow you to compare data more easily.

TALKING ABOUT STATES OF MATTER

You can tell if something is a liquid or not by listening to words. Solids cannot change shape. That means any word like ooze, drip, or pour describes a liquid. Something has to move to ooze, drip, or pour. That means it is changing shape, otherwise it cannot move. It is not alive.

ooze
drip
pour

Words that describe solids are words like hard or firm. Viscosity can also be told through words. If something oozes, it moves slowly. That is how you know it is a more viscous liquid, but not a solid.

CHANGING STATES OF MATTER

Water is known for changing phases. Water can be liquid when you drink it. It can be solid when frozen as ice. It can also be a gas when it is boiled into steam. Steam is also called water vapor.

Matter can change because of the temperature. All atoms <u>vibrate</u>. In solids, they do not vibrate much. In gases, they vibrate a lot. The hotter matter gets, the more the atoms vibrate. If atoms vibrate enough, it can cause them to break some or all of their bonds. Since the bonds hold matter together, these vibrations can change the state of matter.

Thermal Expansion of Solids

Particles Before Heat

- Vibrate a little
- Atoms in fixed positions

Particles After Heat

- Increased kinetic energy vibrations
- Expanded space between atoms
- Vibrate around a fixed position

Changes of phases of matter
0°C
Freezing/Melting point
≈20°C
Room temperature
100°C
Boiling point

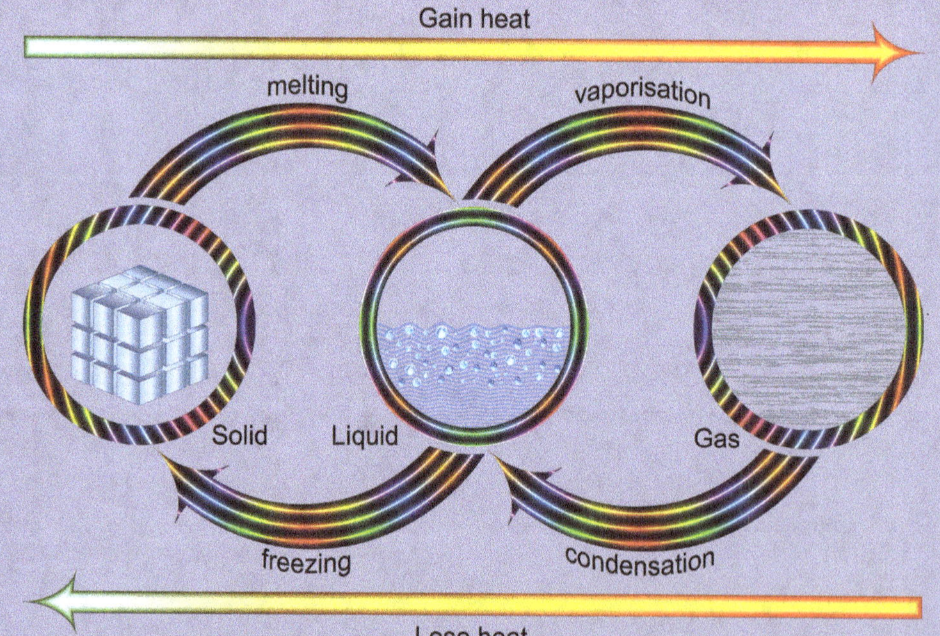
Gain heat
melting
vaporisation
Solid
Liquid
Gas
freezing
condensation
Lose heat

The temperature where a liquid becomes gas is called the boiling point. Gas can also turn back into liquid when it becomes colder. This is called condensation. The temperature where liquids turn to solids is called the freezing point. When it gets warmer, solids can return to liquids. This is the melting point. The boiling, melting, and freezing points change depending on the type of matter.

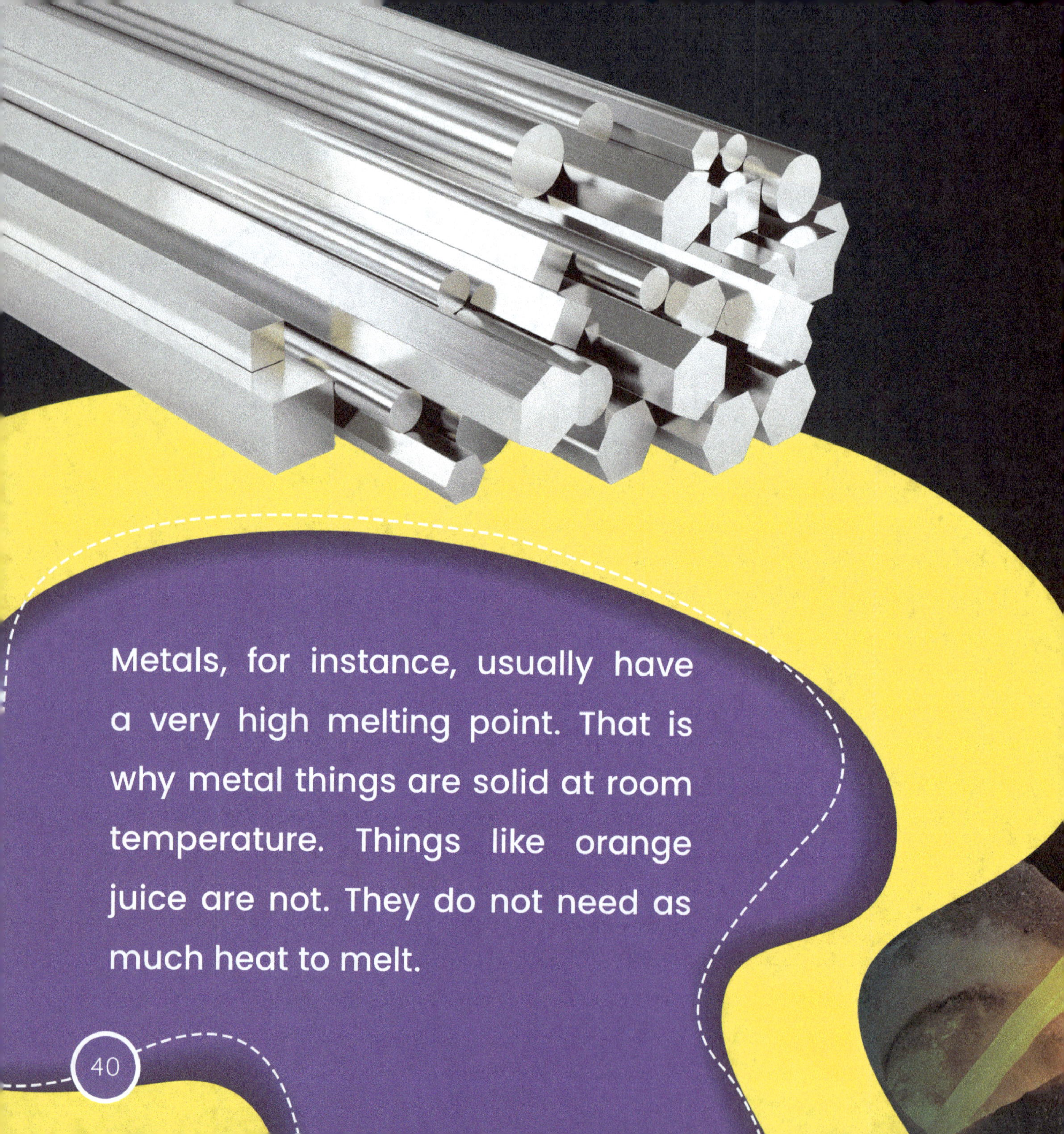

Metals, for instance, usually have a very high melting point. That is why metal things are solid at room temperature. Things like orange juice are not. They do not need as much heat to melt.

Metal casting process with red high temperature fire

Temperatures

Freezing, Melting, Boiling point and Room temperature comparison in Fahrenheit Celsius Kelvin

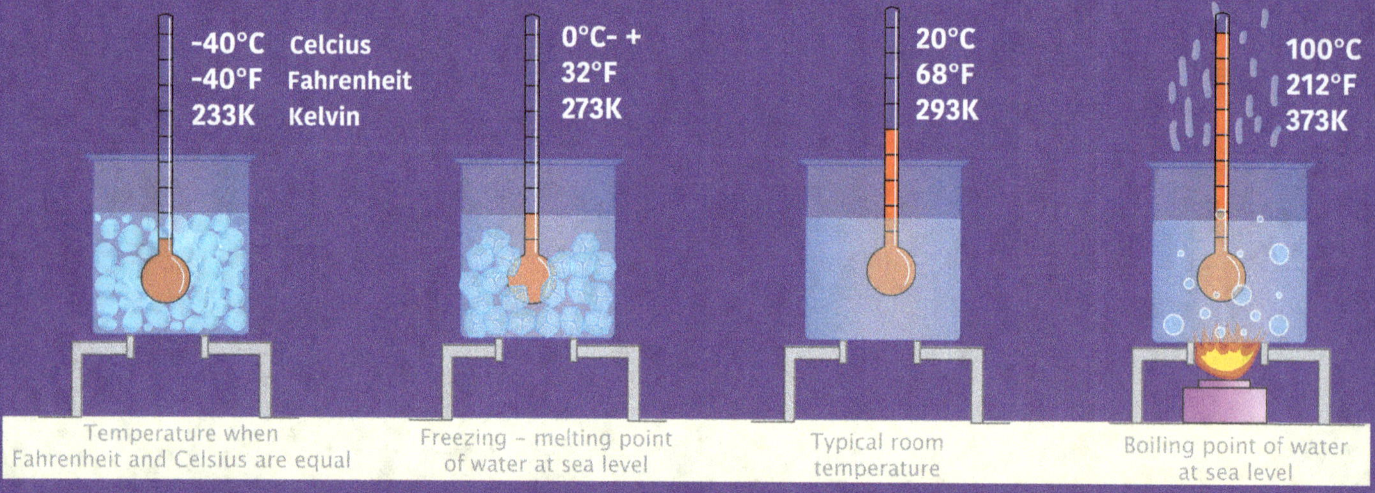

Temperatures in Kelvin, Celsius and Fahrenheit

The melting, boiling, and freezing points do not have to be different temperatures. Water freezes at zero degrees Celsius. This is thirty-two degrees Fahrenheit. Ice also melts at that same temperature. If it has been a very cold day and zero degrees Celsius is the "warmest" recorded temperature, then the accumulated ice will melt. If it were the opposite, then water will freeze at zero degrees Celsius. It depends on the situation.

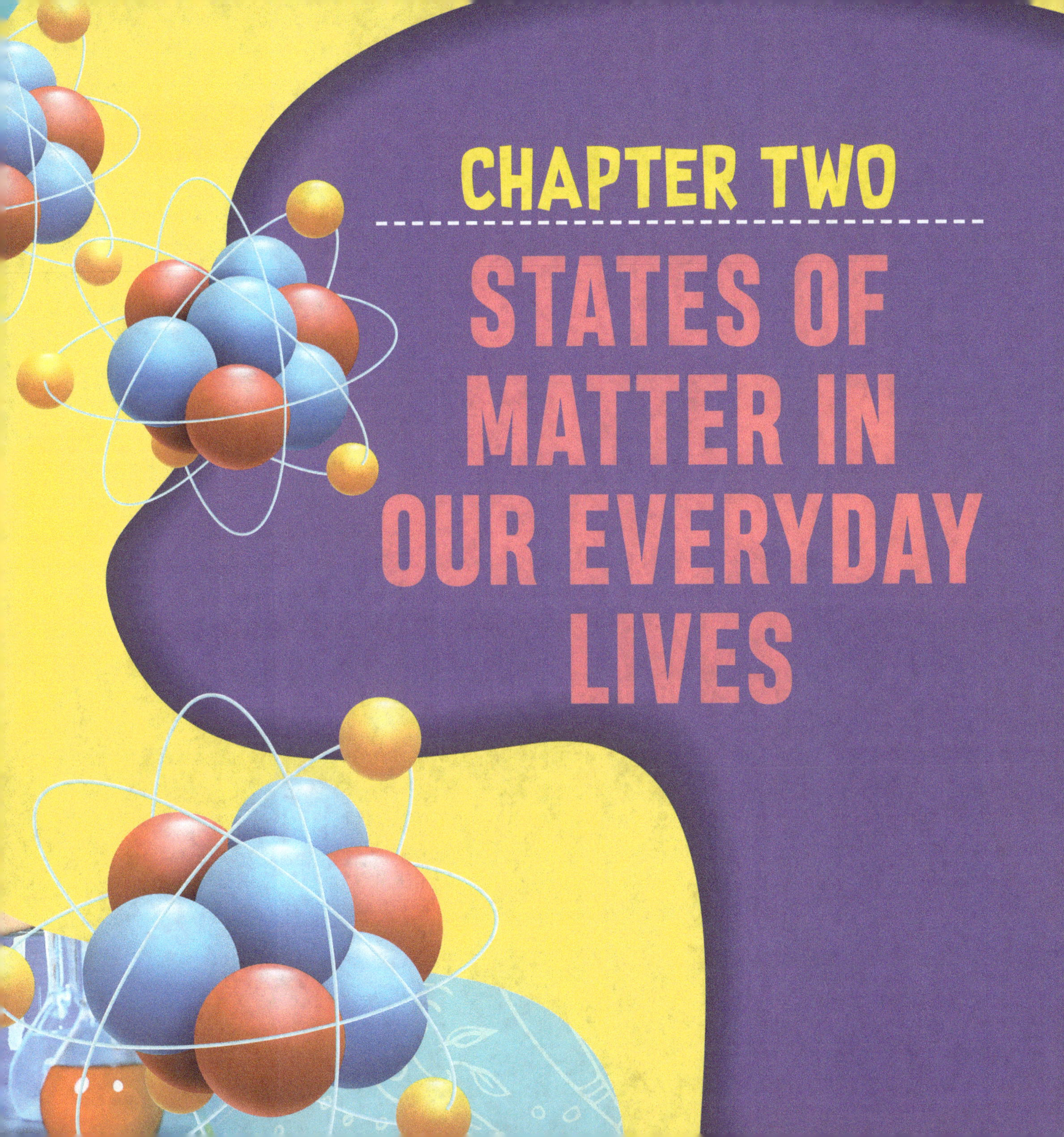

CHAPTER TWO
STATES OF MATTER IN OUR EVERYDAY LIVES

Understanding the different states of matter is important. You should not store a liquid in a container with holes. Gas also cannot be stored in anything with holes. Gases cannot be stored in anything without a lid.

A woman walking on the road

TYPES OF CONTAINERS

Imagine you are cleaning the tank of your pet fish. Your fish needs to be moved to another container. You also need to make certain the water level stays high. That way your fish can swim and breathe.

A man cleaning a fish tank

Fish placed in a container with liquid

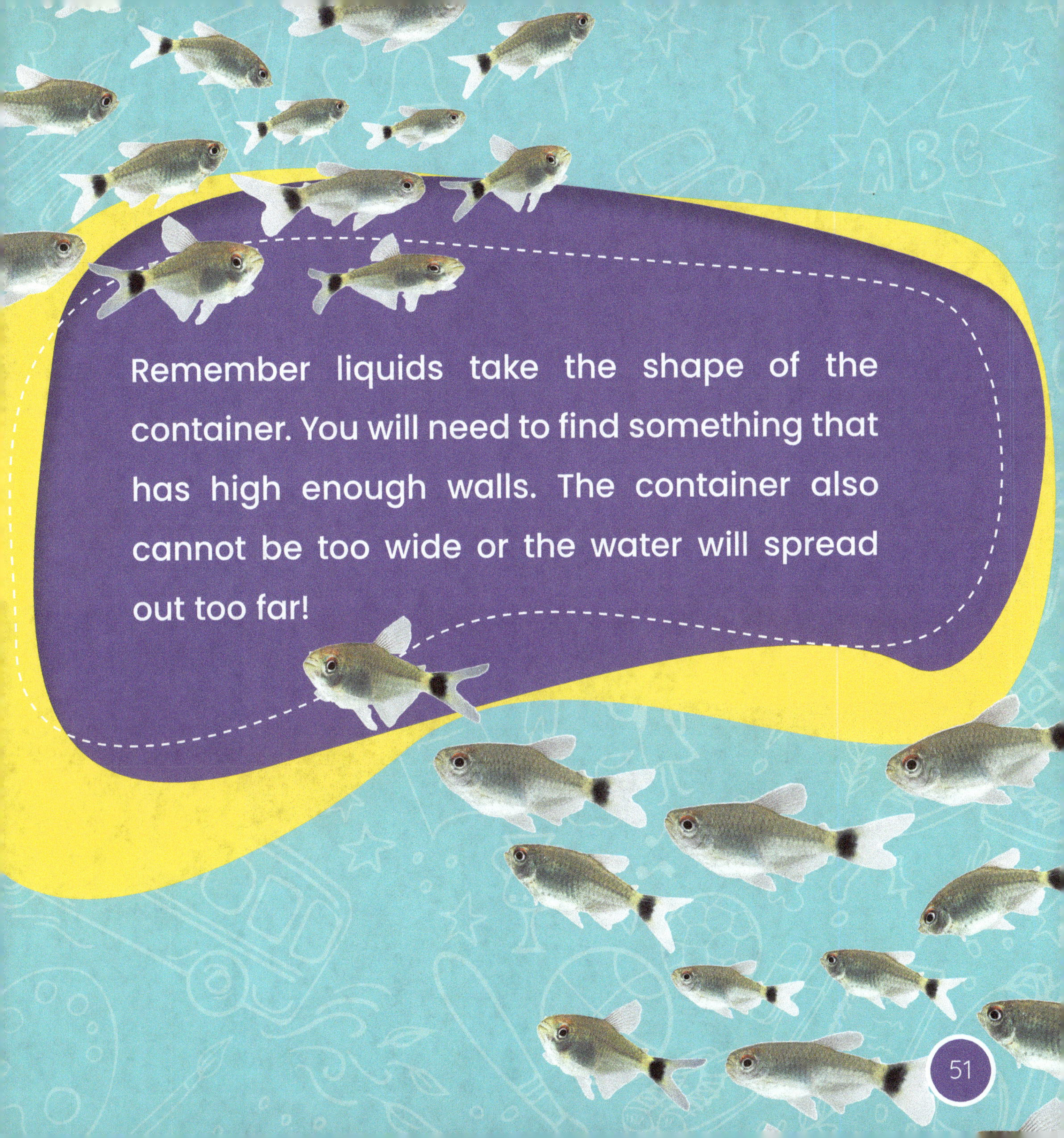

Remember liquids take the shape of the container. You will need to find something that has high enough walls. The container also cannot be too wide or the water will spread out too far!

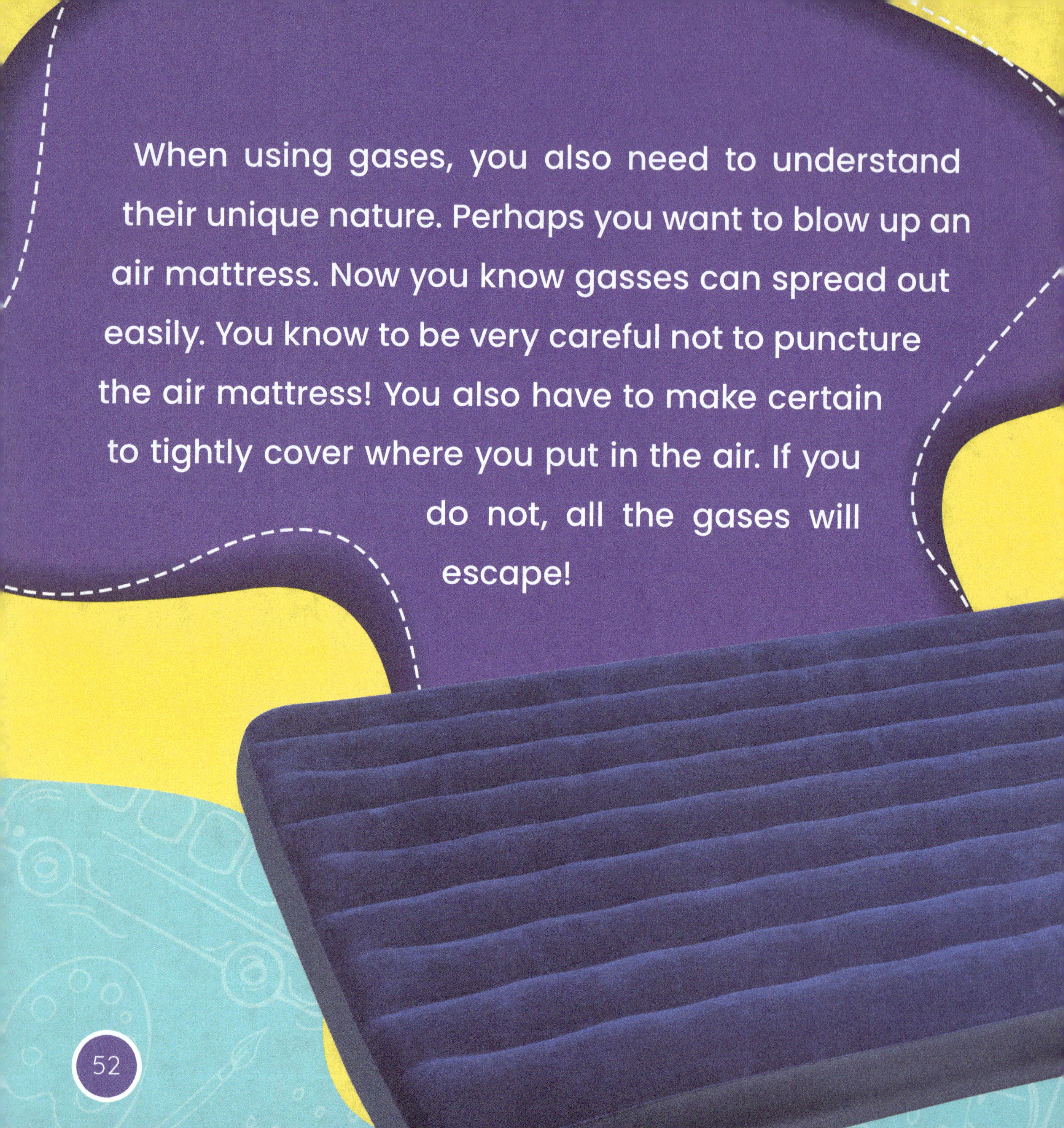

When using gases, you also need to understand their unique nature. Perhaps you want to blow up an air mattress. Now you know gasses can spread out easily. You know to be very careful not to puncture the air mattress! You also have to make certain to tightly cover where you put in the air. If you do not, all the gases will escape!

A woman pumping air into an inflatable mattress.

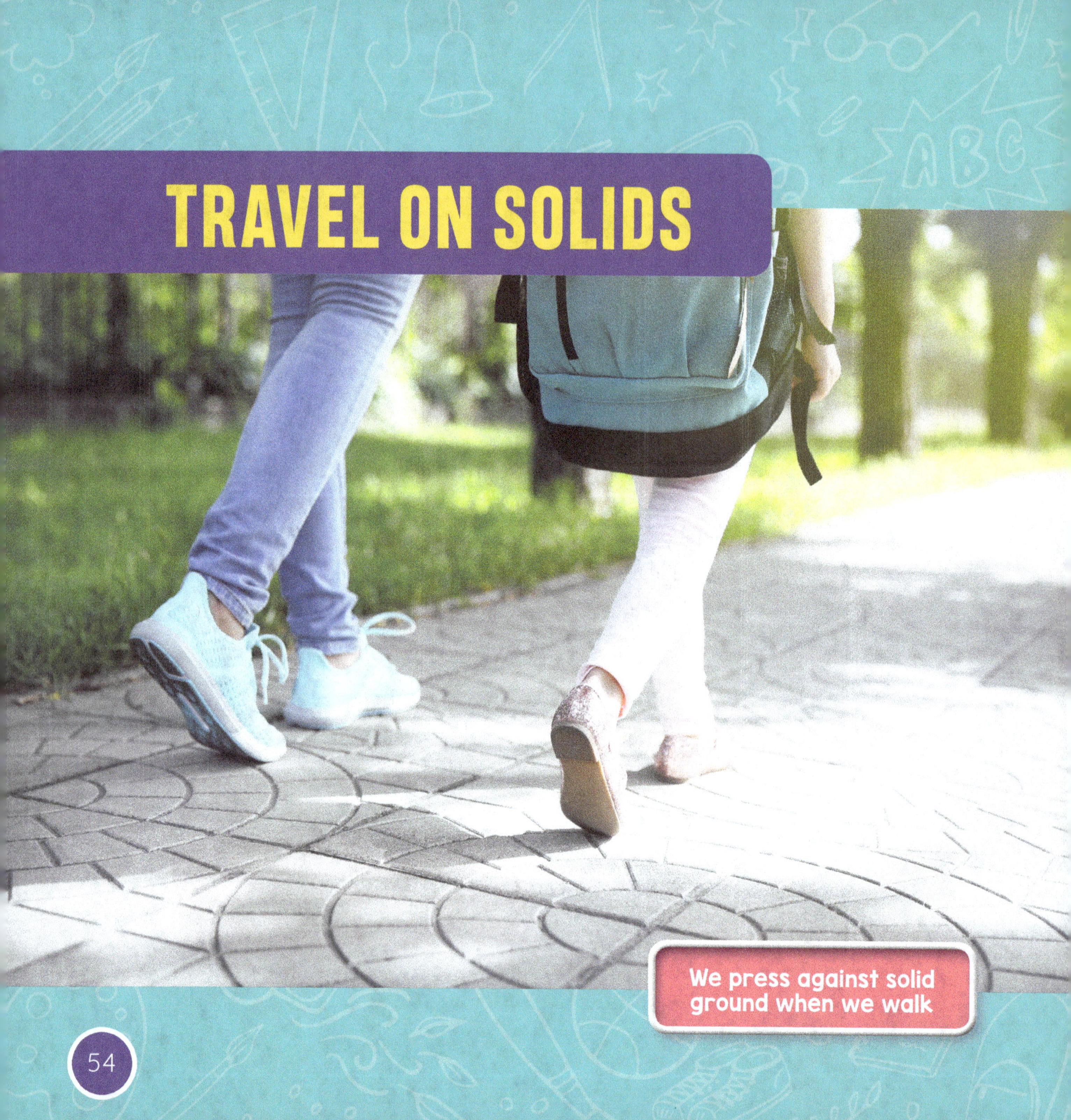

TRAVEL ON SOLIDS

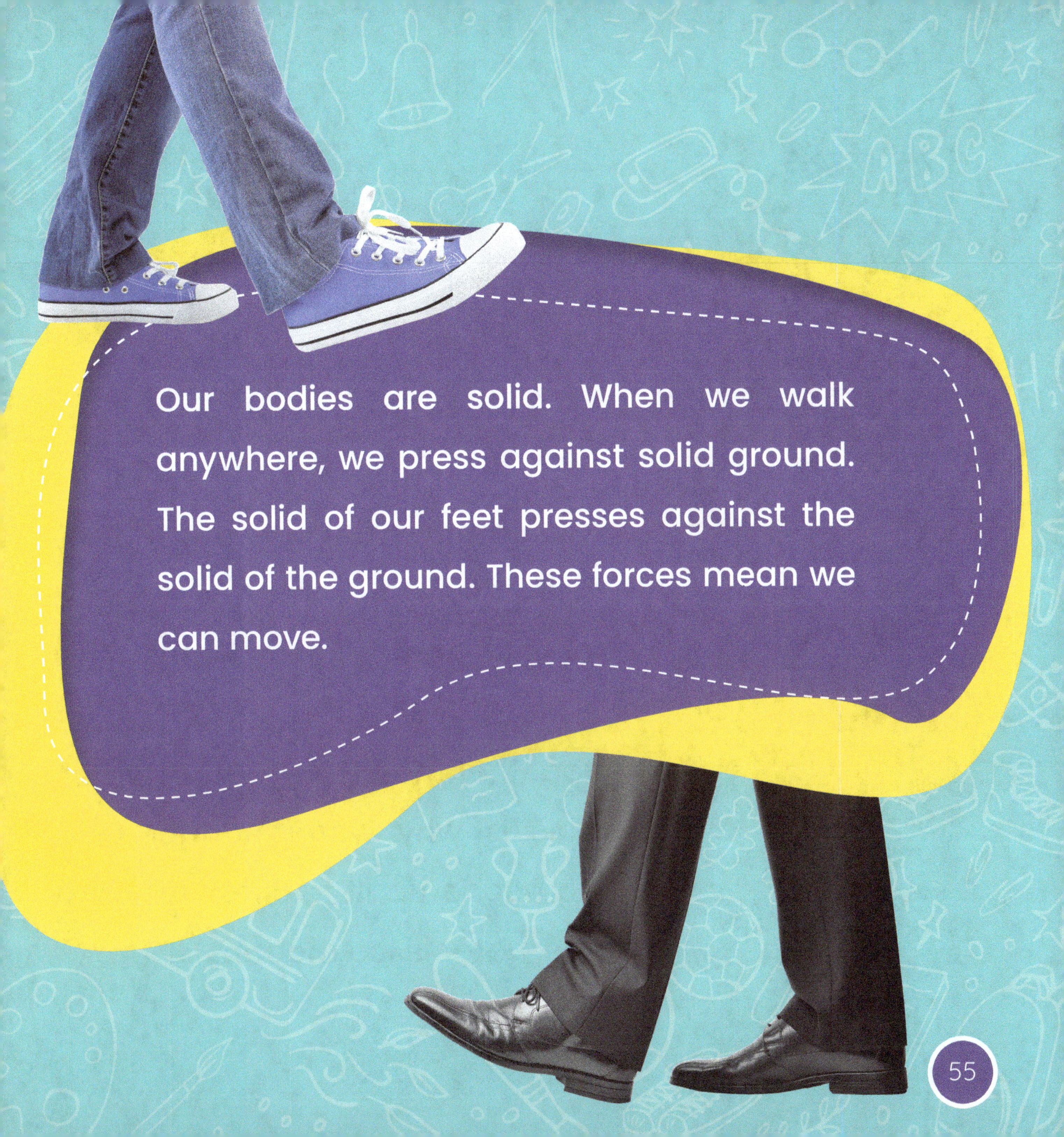

Our bodies are solid. When we walk anywhere, we press against solid ground. The solid of our feet presses against the solid of the ground. These forces mean we can move.

We can walk on frozen water

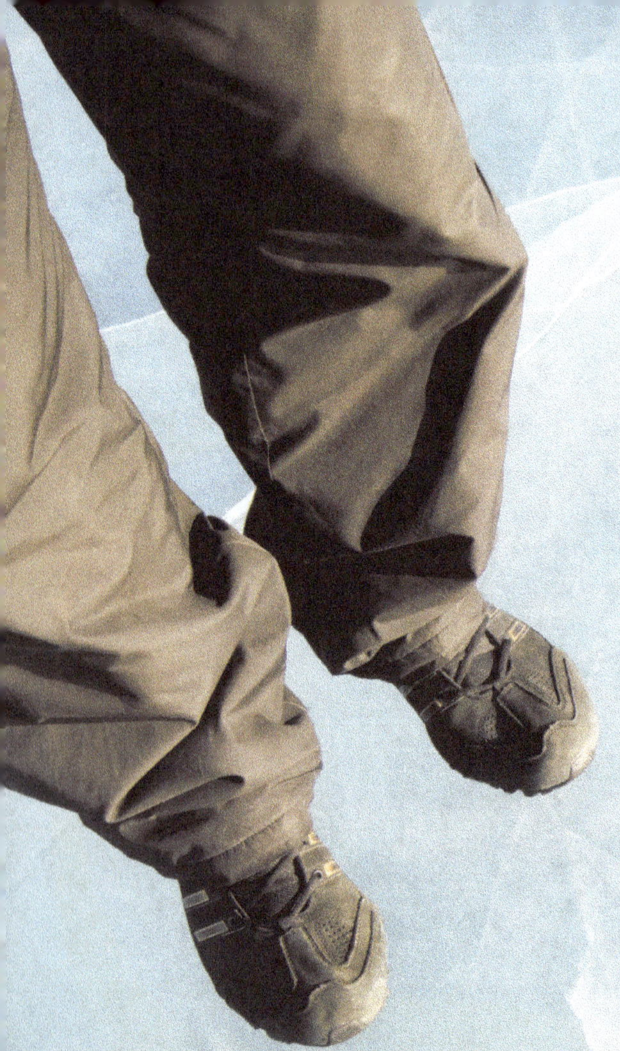

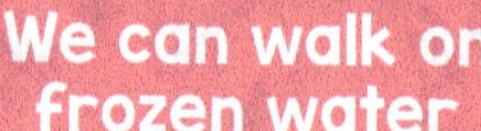

We cannot walk on water unless it is frozen. A human walking is denser than liquid water. This means our atoms are closer together than the atoms in water. This is why water cannot hold someone up. It is different when the water is ice though.

The atoms in water are closer together when frozen. On ice, people can use skates to move. On snow, people can use sleds.

It is also faster to travel by car than to travel by foot. Cars travel best on roads like highways. Roads are smooth and hard meaning cars can move easily. Bikes and skateboards can also do well on roads. The material matters.

Travelling by car
Biking
Skateboarding
59

TRAVEL ON LIQUIDS

People can swim through liquids such as water, but this is not a fast way to travel. Also, if people get tired they can drown. People cannot swim from the United States to the United Kingdom!

60

In order to travel across water, people needed to find a way to travel on liquid. They need things that can float and carry supplies. Ships and boats are how humans can travel on water, even across long distances. If an object is less dense than water, it will float.

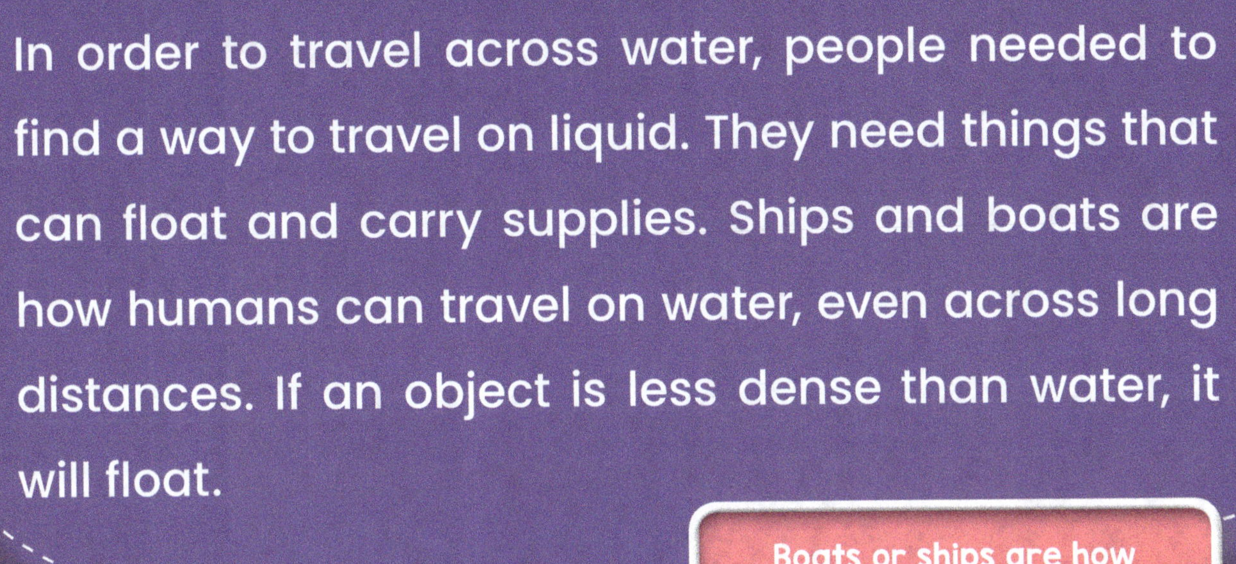

Boats or ships are how humans travel by water

Some ships can be quite heavy and large. They have a lot of mass. This does not stop them from being able to float. If the mass is spread out properly, even something big and heavy can float on water.

People move through the air when they walk. However, if they jump, they fall back down. The air cannot hold their weight. This is because gravity pulls them to the Earth. Everything on Earth is affected by gravity.

If you jump, gravity pulls
you back to the ground.

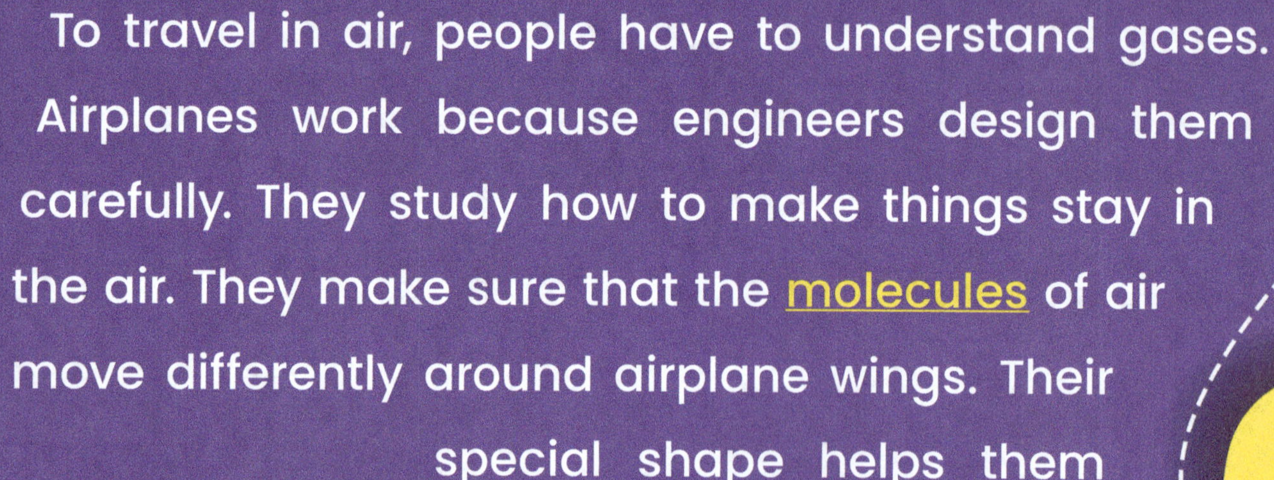

To travel in air, people have to understand gases. Airplanes work because engineers design them carefully. They study how to make things stay in the air. They make sure that the <u>molecules</u> of air move differently around airplane wings. Their special shape helps them stay in the air. There are many forces that allow planes and helicopters to work against gravity.

An airplane's special shape
helps it stay in the air.

Everything in the Universe is made up of matter. Matter is usually found in one of three states: Solid, liquid, or gas. Solids cannot easily change their shape and do not change volume. Liquids change their shape easily, but do not change volume. Gases can change their shape and volume. States of matter can change based on their temperature. Understanding the states of matter can help us. It affects how we use different containers. It also affects how we travel. To learn more about matter, mass, volume, and much more, look for more Baby Professor books!

An illustration of the Universe
that is made up of matter.

GLOSSARY

Particles *(page 4)*: Particles are tiny pieces of matter.

Unique *(page 5)*: Something that is unique is special or one of a kind.

Container *(page 10)*: something that is made to hold another object

Phase *(page 33)*: a form, type, or aspect of something

Vibrate *(page 34)*: to move quickly, back and forth, in one place

Molecules *(page 63)*: two or more atoms bonded together

Visit

www.speedypublishing.com

To view and download free content on your favorite subject and browse
our catalog of new and exciting books for readers of all ages.

www.ingramcontent.com/pod-product-compliance
Lightning Source LLC
Chambersburg PA
CBHW080403030726
47601CB00003B/223